GW01454382

Published by Moleskine SpA

Lettering and Illustrations by
Cyril Vouilloz aka Rylsee

Publishing Director
Roberto Di Puma

Editing and Graphic Design
Luca Bogoni

Texts by
John Z. Komurki

Assistant to the Artist
Memo Vithana

Text Editing
John Z. Komurki and Bertha de Bruyn

ISBN 978-88-6613-161-8

First edition 2017

Printed in Italy by Galli Thierry Stampa

HOW TO PLAY WITH LETTERS

Rylsee

Cyril Vouilloz

Table of Contents

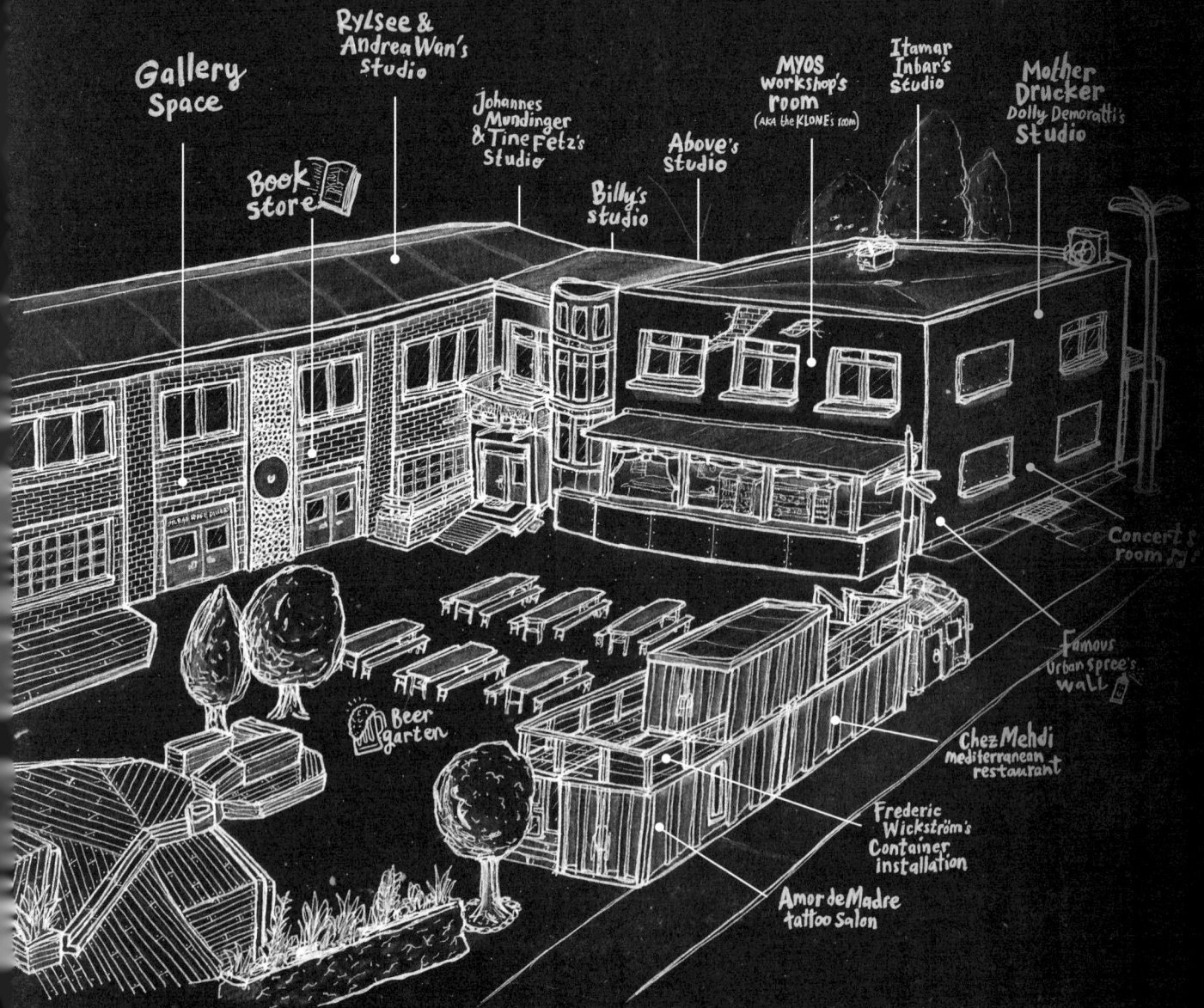

URBAN SPREE
Berlin

Gallery Space

Book store

Rylsee & Andrea Wan's studio

Johannes Mundinger & Tine Fetz's Studio

Billy's studio

Above's studio

MYOS workshop's room (aka the KLONE's room)

Itamar Inbar's studio

Mother Drucker Dolly Demoratti's Studio

Concert's room

Famous Urban spree's wall

Chez Mehdi Mediterranean restaurant

Frederic Wickström's Container installation

Amor de Madre tattoo salon

Beer garten

Foreword

———————

Pascal Feucher
Urban Spree, Berlin
January 2017

Rooted in graffiti and skateboarding, infused by Hip Hop, Rylsee's universe is cool fantasy supplemented by a sharp sense of composition and balance.

His notorious sketchbooks show his everyday practice of thinking up catchy sentences and creating new styles and fonts. Unlike in classical calligraphy, his letters become glitchy, virused, distorted, sped up, melted, remixed, giving rise to a 'dystorpic' universe.

Something that exists on another level of perception, intertwined, assembled and dismantled by the will of a typographer who blurs the lines of reality and creates his own calligraphic spell.

Rylsee recycles his everyday experiences and thoughts and turns them into proverbial low-fi sentences like 'Never trust someone who doesn't like pizza' or 'Too shy to rap', to name only two. Analogue truths for the digital age. Or Fornever.

Using only his drawing skills, Rylsee becomes the modern alchemist, plotting optical illusions in 2D that look like native 3D. In Rylsee's universe, 2D and 3D coalesce, but the craftsman and the maker of illusions take the lead. His 3D is analogue.

Rylsee's passion for devising smart schemes is matched by an equally strong drive to communicate his art – through regular workshops, tutorials and media posts.

If drawings and letters come first, ultimately the artist expands his visions through large woodwork installations and huge wall paintings, enabling the art to incarnate and be seen by the public. Street art and graffiti are an essential part of Rylsee's art, adding scale and grandeur on the one side, and subversion on the other.

I've known Cyril for almost five years. Our Berlin story started at the same time, in the same place. As a resident artist of Urban Spree since the very beginning of the adventure, and through his countless contributions, Rylsee has become more than a friend: he is family.

I'm proud and honoured to introduce the reader to Rylsee's universe.

Cyril Vouilloz aka Rylsee

How to play with letters

––––––––––

Cyril Vouilloz grew up in a village outside Geneva, Switzerland. He spent his early years the way small-town kids do, "skating, blazing, and chilling with friends." But one thing set Cyril apart from his peers: he was always drawing. A hyperactive child, his mum would give him pen and paper when he acted up, and he would spend hours happily absorbed in his creations.

And he never looked back. Cyril started drawing and sketching non-stop, as he does to this day. His style was distinctive from the first. He has always been interested in letters and symbols, remembering how he used to draw different logos from memory: "I just liked their shape, the letters, colours and forms." But a watershed moment came in his teenage years, when a member of a local graffiti crew glimpsed his sketchbooks. He was invited to start painting his designs on walls, and he acquired the moniker Rylsee, an inversion of his birth name in the style of French street slang (Cyril > Rilcy > Rylsee). Graffiti is what Rylsee spent the next ten years doing, developing his art, traveling, and laying the foundations for the style that would win him followers around the world.

Rylsee the graffiti writer was distinguished by his 'left hand style' (as it happens, Rylsee is a proud southpaw). Not wanting to limit himself to repeating the same letters and shapes in a traditional tag, he mixed up letters and illustration in zany configurations.

8

This style – "awkward and goofy-looking, but with thought behind it," in his own words – has since become popular in the graffiti scene, but back then it wasn't widely respected, and some of his pieces were even slashed out.

The next watershed came in 2011. Rylsee was in Vancouver, working in the renowned Red Gate project, when he decided he needed a new challenge. So, after four months in São Paulo, Brazil, he relocated to Berlin, just in time to get on board with the now legendary Urban Spree project. Urban Spree is a sprawling post-industrial space in the Friedrichshain neighbourhood, old warehouses interspersed with offices, shipping crates and, in the summer, a beer garden. Transformed into a hub for art and music, in a few years this unique space established itself at the heart of Berlin's alternative art scene and, as its first and most prominent creator-in-residence, as well as the man responsible for much of the project's graphic identity, Rylsee is an integral member of the collective.

He takes grim pleasure in remembering the hardships and camaraderie of the first year: broken windows, no heating, no running water. Things have changed since then. Today Urban Spree hosts many different spaces, among them the Urban Spree Galerie, an independent art space that works mainly with street and graffiti artists, and its flagship 'Artist Wall', overlooked by busy Warschauer Strasse; a Bookshop, specialized in urban culture, screen printing and zines; a dedicated Concert Room; and the renowned Mother Drucker screen print studio. Alongside all this, the complex regularly hosts festivals, events and workshops. (Sadly, in 2019 Urban Spree will be claimed by the wave of gentrification inexorably sweeping across Berlin, and all that space will be filled with condos.)

The lifeblood of Urban Spree is its artist residencies, which enable creatives from all over the world to come and set up permanent, medium or short term projects. The current roster includes Andrea Wan, Tavar Zawacki (a.k.a. Above), Johannes Mundinger, Tine Fetz, Billy, and master printer Dolly Demoratti at Mother Drucker. As the project's first artist in residence, Ryslee was able to contribute to defining the spirit of the programme. His influence is everywhere, both graphically and in terms of how the space works.

Don't make the mistake of labelling him an artist, though. He is careful to keep it vague ("even I don't know exactly what I'm doing"), maintaining that he works with letters (but doesn't do hand lettering or typography) and illustration (but not design, as such). It is this shifting, hybrid status that makes him such an interesting and unpretentious creator. "My work is simple," he says, "I talk about things from daily life, about the things that surround me.

I like the idea I can create something that makes someone laugh on the other side of the world."

Rylsee's huge success on Instagram is partly attributable to this simplicity and accessibility. But don't be deceived – the shiny surface conceals hidden depths, and Rylsee's work is always multifaceted. He explains his success on Instagram and other social media in terms of having something for everyone:

designers will appreciate the composition and visual balance of his pieces; typography nerds will enjoy the subtle riffs on font construction; a non-artistic public will appreciate the humour and message; and his granny would say, "it's very nice Cyril, but don't you think you should add colours?"

This book tries to offer an insight into all the many facets of Rylsee's work. You will find a dazzling range of different experiments, from trompe l'oeil photography to painstakingly rendered gallery pieces. One particularly distinctive characteristic of his work is his analogue rendering of digital 'glitch' effects – letters are warped, twisted, melted almost beyond legibility, like skew-whiff Xeroxes or bad code, only hand-drawn. This is very far from a gimmick. Rather than simply tracing these effects, Rylsee studies them deeply, trying to understand where, how and why the letters get glitched. The result is at times baffling, at times unsettling, but always stimulating and provocative, right on the fault line that divides digital and analogue art.

Rylsee has a complex relation to digital creation. "I'm fascinated by the digital but, in the end, it doesn't exist," he says. "It's beautiful, but there's no physical reality." One of the many paradoxes of his work is precisely that he painstakingly and deliberately replicates effects that in their original context are read as mistakes. A human copying a computer's errors, and at the same time embellishing them, injecting them with soul: "the magic is in the imperfections."

Another defining aspect of Rylsee's aesthetic is a very contemporary emphasis on process rather than end result. "We should embrace the fact that people do something, rather than judge the final product." For him, "well done doesn't mean interesting" – the idea is everything. This ethos is encapsulated in his almost obsessive use of sketchbooks. He is never without one, and these infinitely inventive compendia are the key to Rylsee's aesthetic. Like so much of what he does, they are impossible to classify – are the notebooks the source or the finished work? Are they the fruit or the root of his creativity?

Rylsee's art throws off these questions like sparks, all of them equally tricky to answer. Constantly shifting, surprising, challenging, his vision is programmatically hybrid. Rylsee's world is a wonderful place to be.

Heartless
ONCE
CARED
TOO MUCH

Heartless
ONCE
CARED
TOO MUCH

TH♡SE
WHO ARE
Heartless
ONCE
Cared
TOO MUCH

Those HOW
ARE
Heartless
ONCE CARED
Too much

THOSE
HOW
ARE
Heartless
Once cared
TOO MUCH

"Stay simple stay honest."

SLOGANS, MOTTOS & PUNCHLINES

Rylsee is (in)famous for his use of short phrases and slogans. Drawing inspiration from modern life, he comes up with ready-made catchphrases that puncture the superficiality of smartphone culture. Only short, punchy expressions cut through the fog of information overload. Rylsee channels their impact, turning it to his own playful or subversive ends. He sketches these phrases and then works some of them up into bigger pieces, from stickers to murals.

Fusing skewed New Age wisdom and stoner gags, his throwaway phrases and slogans are sometimes witty, sometimes silly, always provocative. From his sketchbooks to the subway walls – via that staple of the street artist's practice, the impossi-ble-to-peel-off sticker – Rylsee preaches. His words share the same immediacy as graffiti, advertising or political sloganeering, but his philosophy takes longer to sink in, and this combination of power and subtlety is partly responsible for his success in transcending cultural boundaries.

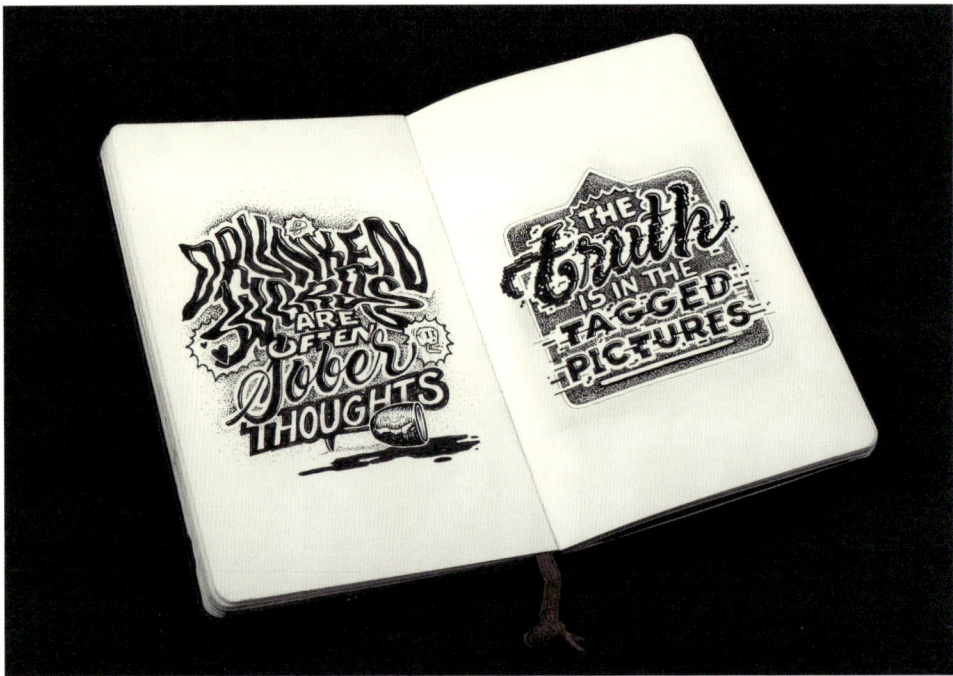

PIZZA: A cornerstone of Rylsee's life philosophy.

DRUNKEN WORDS: Rylsee saw this slogan scribbled on the wall of the toilets in the Urban Spree concert venue.

TAKE YOUR TIME: "This is a note to myself," Rylsee says. "I tend to pressure myself to do more, more, more. So this is a friendly reminder."

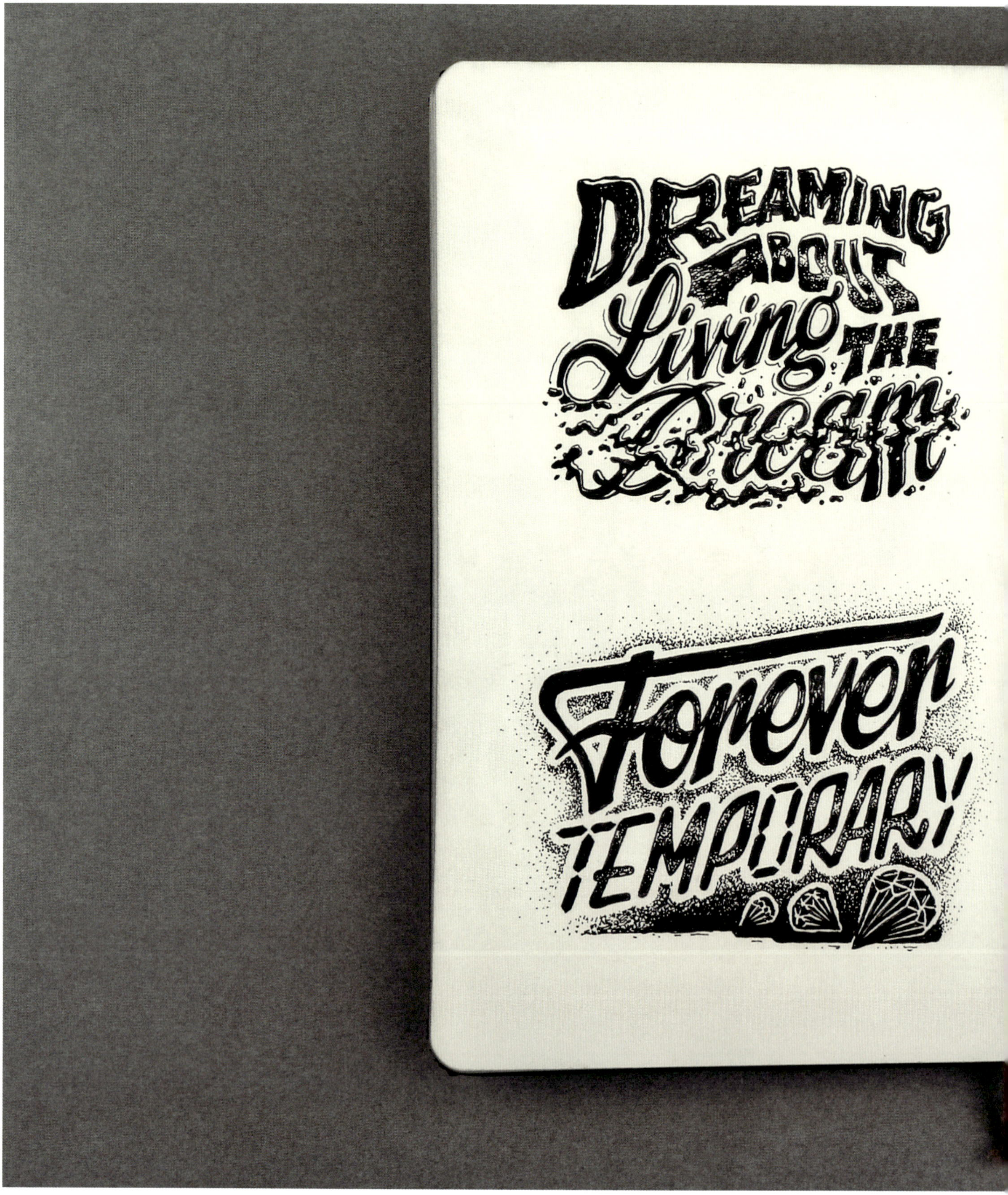
DREAMING ABOUT Living THE Dream
Forever TEMPORARY

LET'S FORGET WHAT WE *Can't* REMEMBER

WHAT'S YOUR FAVORITE PROCRASTINATION ACTIVITY ???

Too shy to rap

———

Year: 2013
Location: Berlin, Geneva
Materials: Paper, Ink, Stickers

One of Rylsee's most well-known interventions is a sticker that says TOO SHY TO RAP. Written in flamboyant bubble letters and printed on shiny eggshell, it raises a smile at the thought of the nerdy artist who is too shy to share his love for Hip Hop except via anonymous messages. But go beyond the words themselves, and examine what else the creator is trying to say. What does it mean that someone is too shy to rap? Why should shyness be an impediment to expressing yourself? With this slogan Rylsee uses the stylized language of graffiti to critique the brash, macho posturing at the heart of many street style cultures. And there is a sense, too, that it is the artist himself who is too shy to rap – his art is the only way he can play with words.

SMART PHONE: "This drawing speaks for itself, I think."

MOJITO: This drawing is part of an ongoing series called #MyFollowersQuotes.

IMAGINATION AIRLINES: This composition was Rylsee's contribution to a community drawing challenge.

5AM KEBAB: The inspiration for this piece was a kebab that Rylsee ate on the way home one night/morning: "Even though I knew it was filthy, each bite was filled with magic and happiness."

FIVE WORDS: This drawing was Rylsee's way of inviting his followers to write a comment detailing how to ruin a beautiful moment in only five words.

I THINK my SPiRiT ANiMAL is a Mojito

ITALWAYS FEELS LIKE · THE BEST KEBAB · I'VE EVER HAD WHEN IT IS 5 AM!

CLOSE YOUR EYES & Imagination AIRLINES SINCE ∞ LET YOURSELF TRAVEL SOMEWHERE

RUIN A Beautiful Moment IN Five WORDS

THOSE WHO ARE Heartless Once cared TOO MUCH

THIS BEER TASTE LIKE

THIS BEER taste like I'M NOT GONNE

25

Rylsee has a love/hate relationship with the internet. While he uses it widely for research, work and promotion, he, like all of us, can waste hours and hours scrolling through junk. This is the idea behind the piece 'What did you NOT do today because of the internet?' Rylsee says that "one thing I find interesting is the interaction and exchange that the internet (and especially Instagram) provides." An example of this is a fan's response to 'What did you NOT do today': "The day after I posted it, someone tagged me in a drawing that answered my question: the image was a copy of mine, with the same drawing of a laptop, but on the screen was written: 'I did this!' It always touches me a lot when interactions like this occur."

Rylsee says his internet drawings can be compared to memes: "Some of these drawings, as visually simple as they were, became widely appreciated online. This might be because they speak to issues that every internet / social media user can relate to."

One idea he likes to play with is #nofilter. This is a tag used on Instagram to indicate that a photo is 'raw', and has not had a filter applied to it. With characteristic playfulness, Rylsee applied this idea to a doobie and, as he says, "this silly joke turned out to be another viral drawing."

"I miss my pre-internet brain" is a quote from novelist Douglas Coupland.

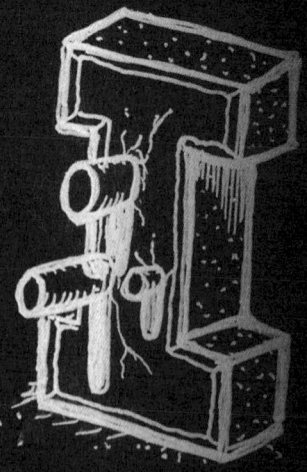

"Typography with soul."

LETTERS & FRIENDS

Rylsee has a very intimate relationship with letters. Evolving out of his youthful fascination with logos and branding, and passing through his apprenticeship as a graffiti writer, this love of letters has expanded and matured, eventually coming to define his style.

On top of his formal and stylistic explorations, Rylsee likes to play with the very nature of letters. In his hands, letters come to life. He imbues them with soul: "I like to imagine the letters doing stuff, having their own activities, their own life." To interact with Rylsee's anthropomorphic interpretations is to see the familiar in a thrillingly new light.

Neither typography nor illustration, Rylsee's menagerie of weird and wonderful letters boggle the mind and expand the imagination. They acquire unexpected dimensions and characteristics – they can come to represent people, objects, even whole buildings. He believes that letters have hidden properties: his job is to share that secret magic with the world.

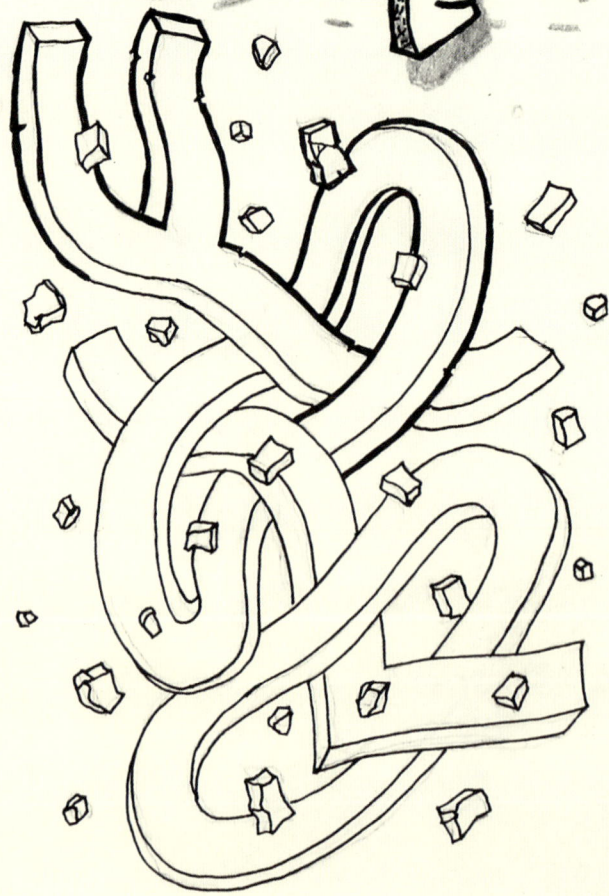

"One day when I was tired of graphical structure, typographical grids, and other structural elements," Rylsee says, "I started the lazy letters series." He decided to draw some letters freehand with "no more pencil constructions or straight lines." This flexibility gives the letters a louche air. "I imagine them chillin'," says the artist. "These are mind-gymnastics for me. Because I do not sketch them, I have to think carefully about each line before tracing it. There's no way back."

People often ask Rylsee how he plans all the proportions of a drawing if he doesn't pencil sketch a structure beforehand. Here's his secret: "Before I even start, I focus hard on the image I want to draw. I think about it until I can visualise it in 3D in my head. When the image is implanted in my mind, I can then 'copy my imagination'. It's a bit like life drawing at school, except that in this case I'm the only one who can see the original image."

These pages were drawn entirely freehand. "If I can hear my drawing make sound," Rylsee says, "that means I'm headed in the right direction."

Guess What Alphabet

Year: 2013
Location: Zimmer, Tel Aviv
Materials: Paper, Ink

For this piece, Rylsee invented a game. Each letter of the alphabet is depicted with certain characteristics or accessories – the game is to guess what each one represents. 'R' is shown with a rope, and 'T' with tape, but other letters are more baffling. What is a 'Y' in fishnet stockings supposed to represent? An 'I' converted into a growhouse? A core goal of *Guess What* was to actively engage viewers. Another was to make viewers engage with each other. For the artist, the best moments were when complete strangers teamed up to figure out what the letters were supposed to depict. Although the originals were conceived in English, in Israel people would find Hebrew words, but in France they would find French ones: an endlessly adaptable game.

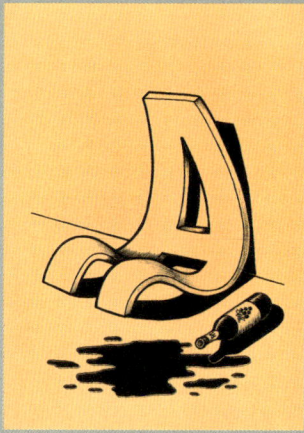
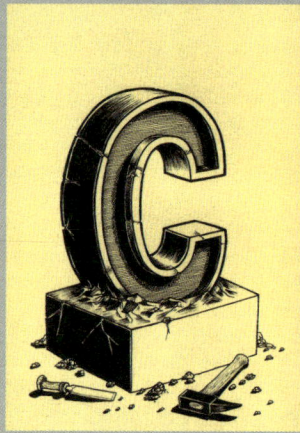
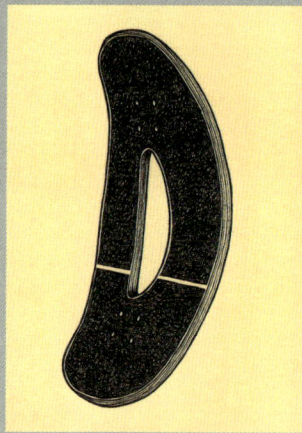
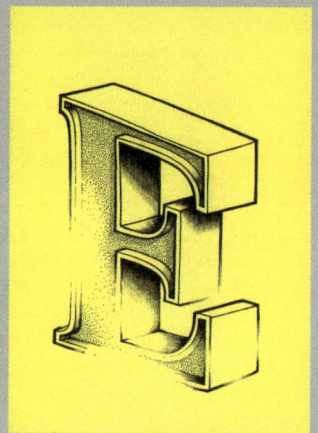
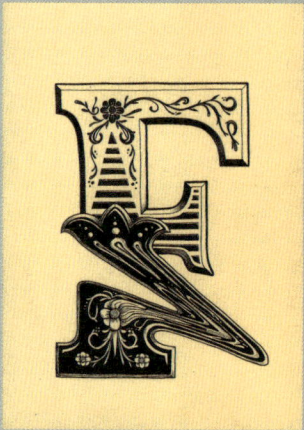

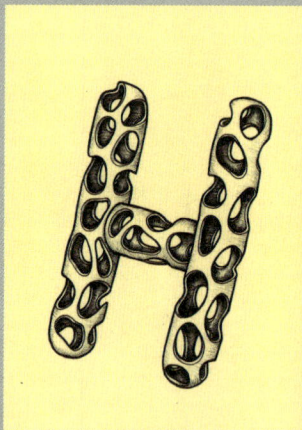

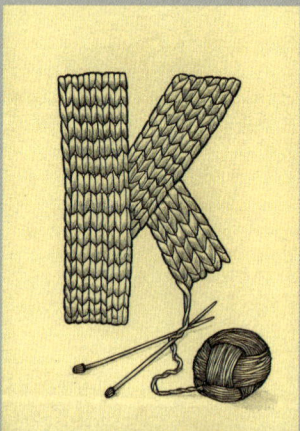

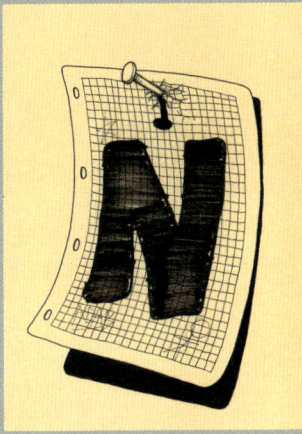
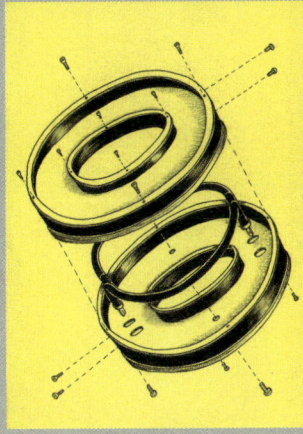
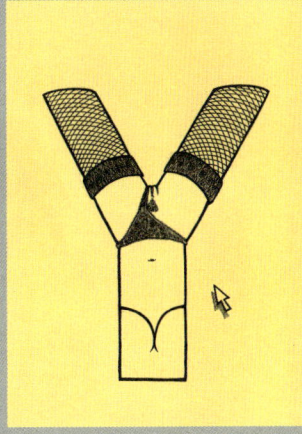
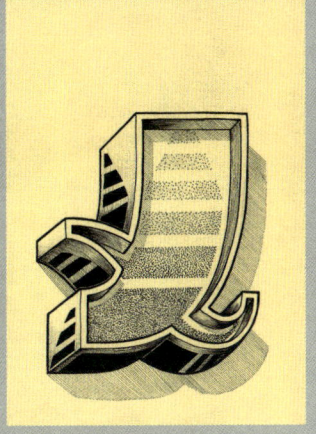
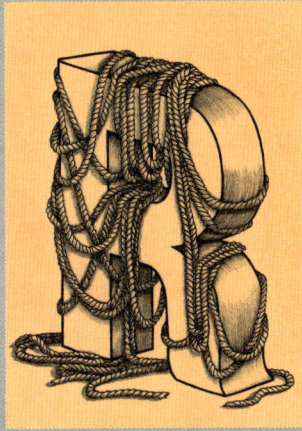
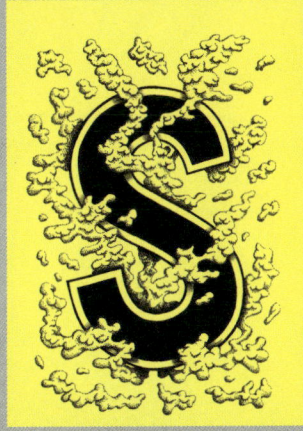

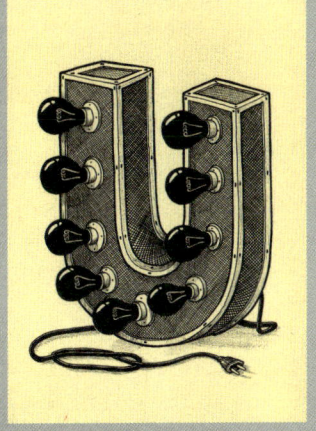

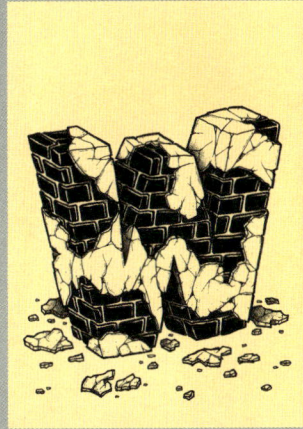
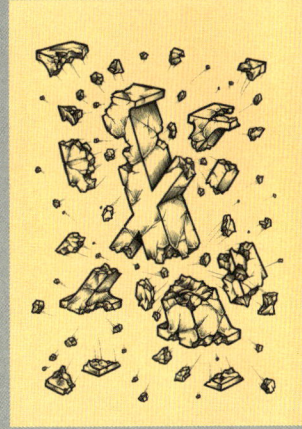

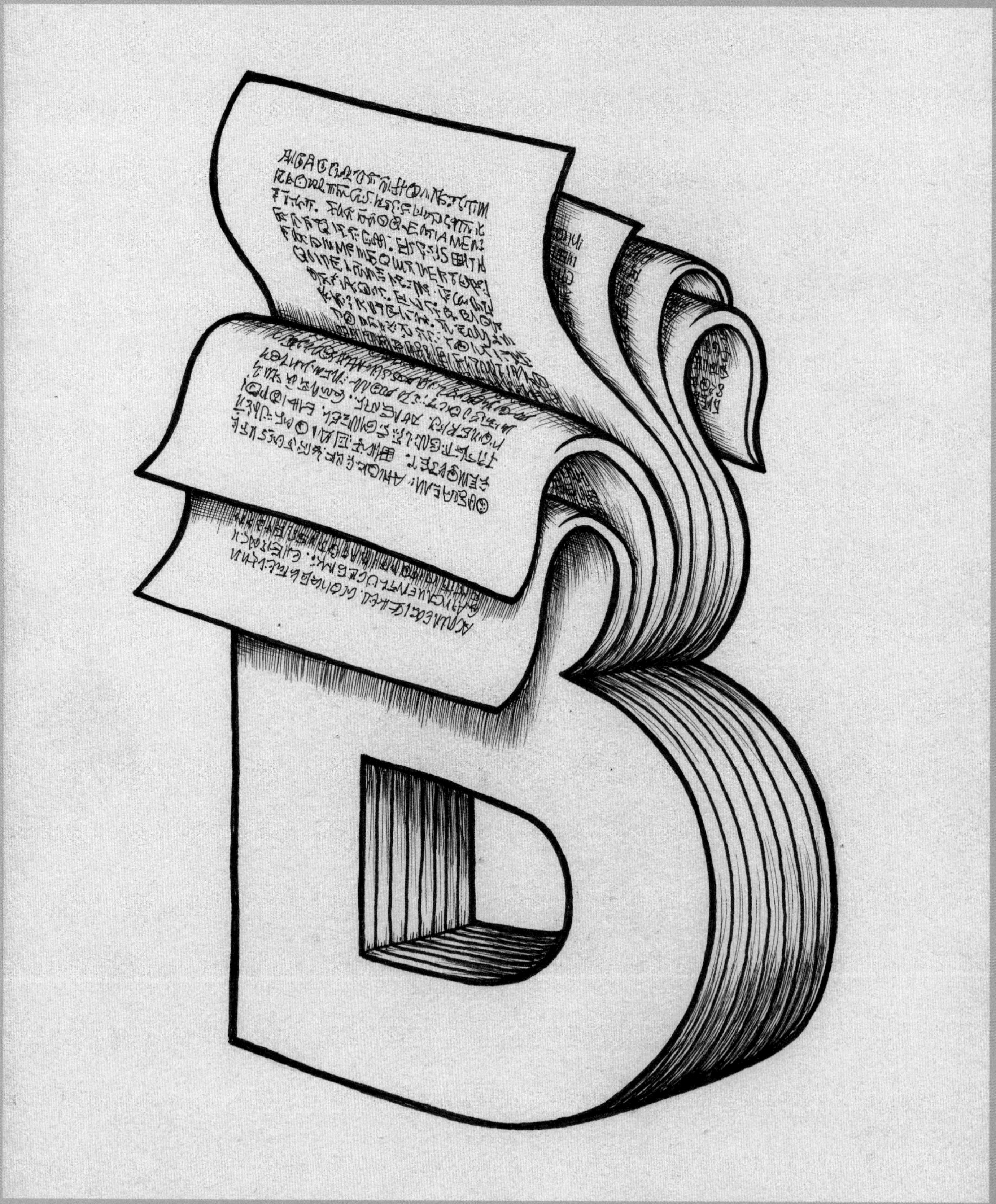

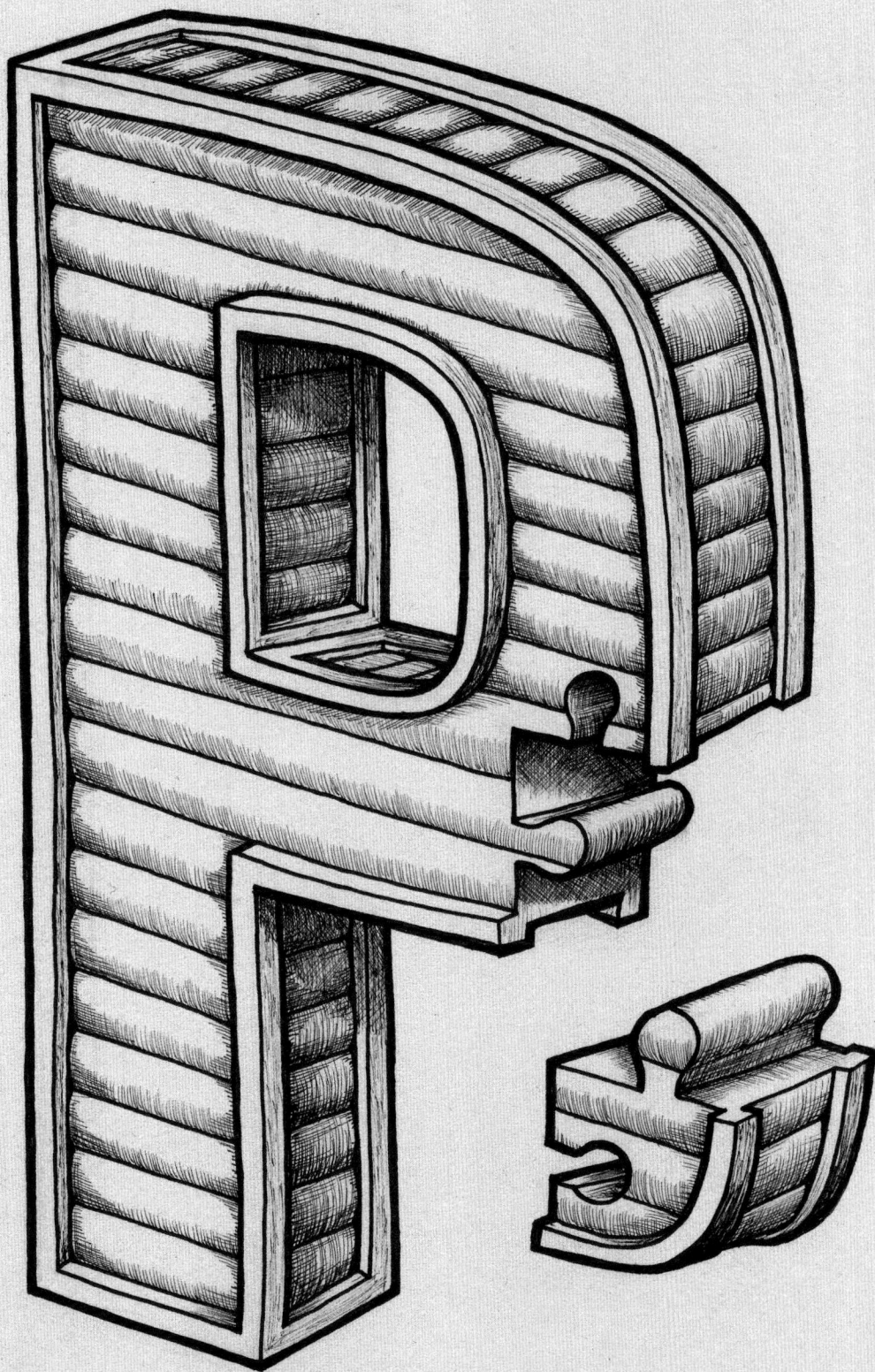

fig.1

BLOCK LETTERS: Let's let Rylsee himself explain the genesis of this series: "The post-apocalyptic marks of time of these constructions is directly inspired by the abandoned places where I like to go and paint sometimes. I like to witness the marks of the time passing on a building. There is a kind of sexiness in decay. I like to imagine how, at some point, these ghost places were populated and lively. It pushes me to tell myself tales about them."

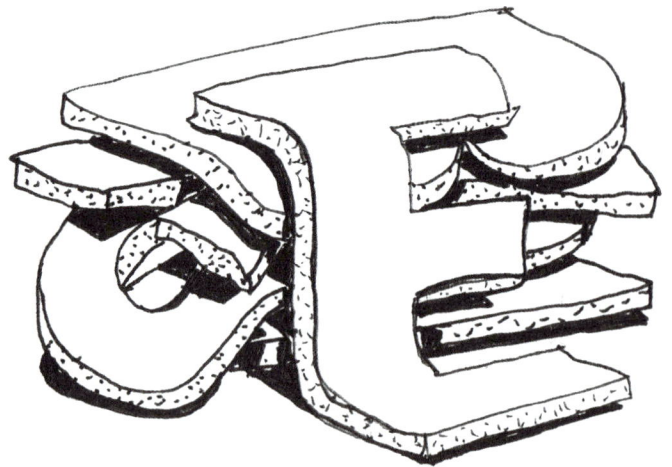

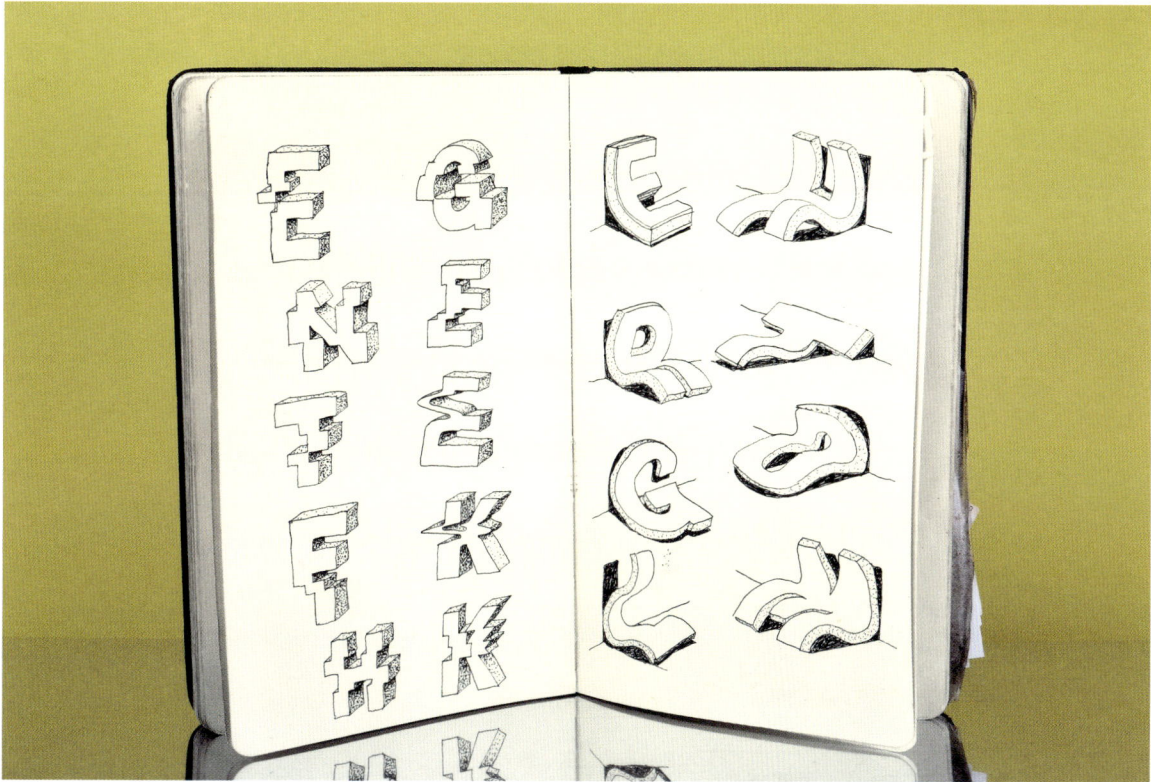

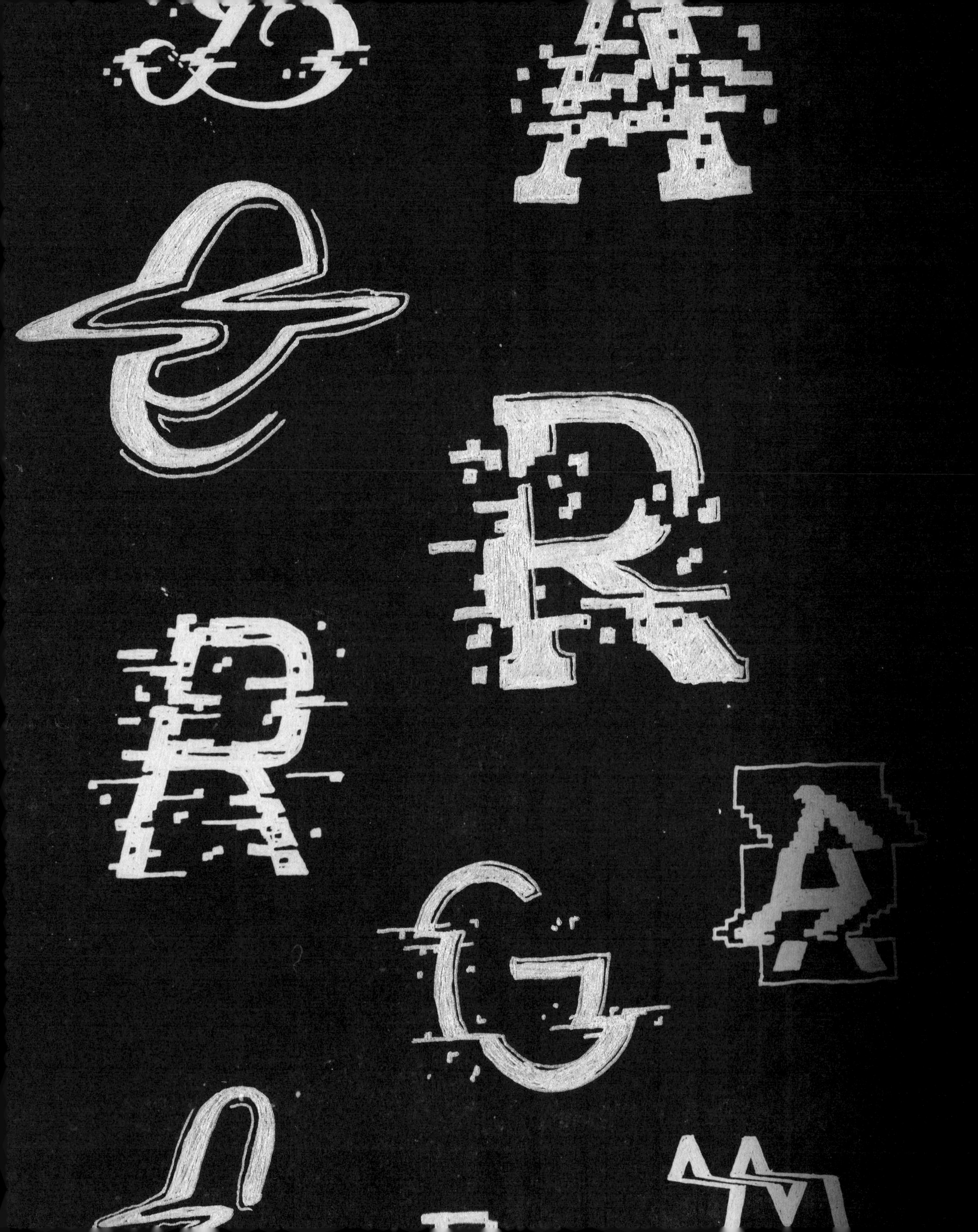

"Perfection isn't sexy".

ANALOGUE GLITCH

What is glitch? In its basic sense, a glitch is a passing malfunction in a digital system. But in the context of art and design, glitch can refer to an aesthetic that plays with flaws in visual processing. Either by copying actual glitches (like those visualization errors that occur when a DVD is scratched) or by using techniques that reproduce the effect at will, artists have explored the disruptive/creative potential of software malfunction. Rylsee is also very interested in glitch effects, but his approach is unique in applying these effects to analogue creation, in a style that has since been much imitated.

"I really like people to ask, how is it done?" Rylsee is known all over the Instasphere for his chopped and screwed aesthetic, as well as his inventiveness in applying digital glitch effects to analogue drawing. As he himself explains, "a lot of my work tricks the viewer. This is my interpretation of what's happening when there's a glitch. I study it, I try to understand how the parts divide and where they multiply, in order to be able to replicate the effect without copying it. Because that's what's interesting in the end. You can take a font and play with it on Illustrator, but it won't have the same effect."

45

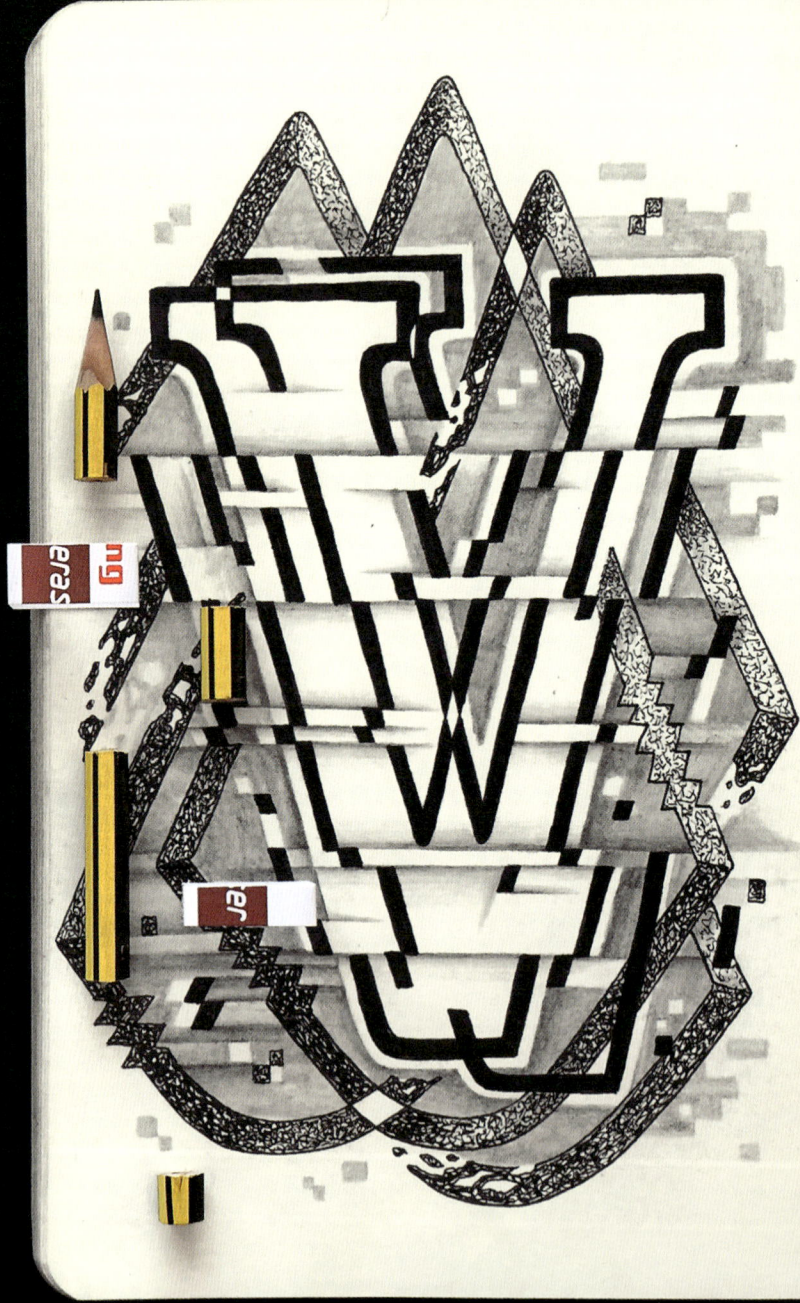

COMMAND V: This, he thinks, is Rylsee's most successful glitch drawing
to date. "This image perturbs the eye
because of the dynamic of the composition. Your eyes can't find anywhere
to settle, so there's no rest for
them." The inspiration came when he
was clearing up after a workshop, and
came to a table with an interesting
arrangement of pencils and erasers.
"The effect of repetition was really
interesting so I decided to try to
make a composition with it. I started
to cut parts of pencils and erasers
and played around with it until the
final photo looked like an actual
computer glitch."

Dystorpia series

———————

Year: 2014 – ongoing
Location: Hamburg, Berlin, Brussels
Materials: Ply Wood, Acrylic

The DYSTORPIA series represents the fullest and most complex expression to date of one of Rylsee's abiding manias: hand-rendered glitch effects. DYSTORPIA started as an exploration of technological problems such as pixel or image distortions, and expanded into a piece that plays with the viewer's eye, appearing to warp 3D space. The different pieces in the series are so visually perplexing that they bodily draw people in and then push them away – to try and 'read' DYSTORPIA becomes an existential rite. The most recent incarnation of DYSTORPIA was as Rylsee's contributions to the 2016 Urban Spree group shows in Berlin and Brussels.

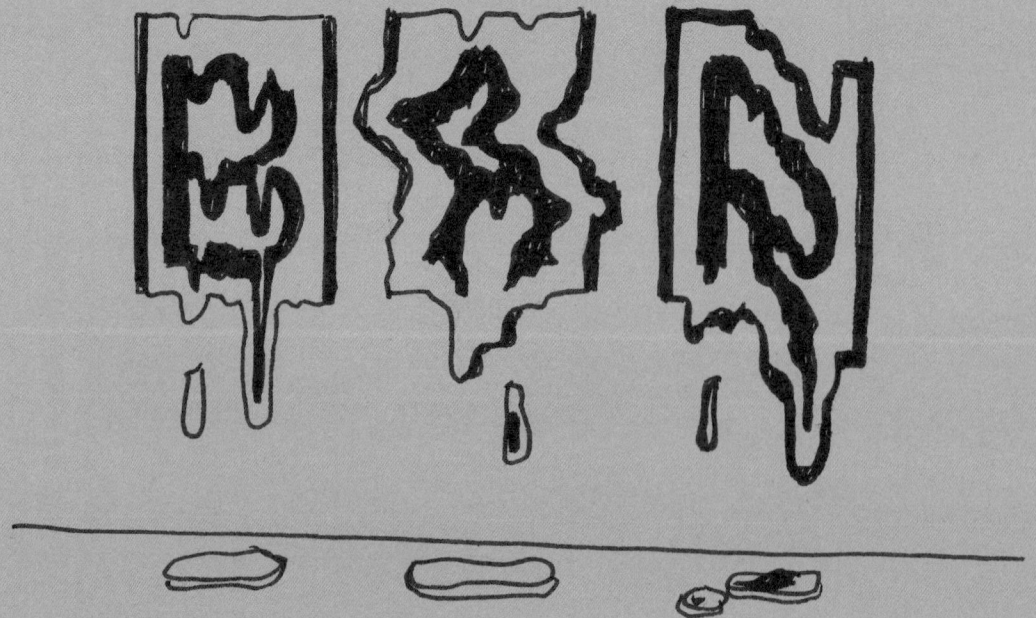

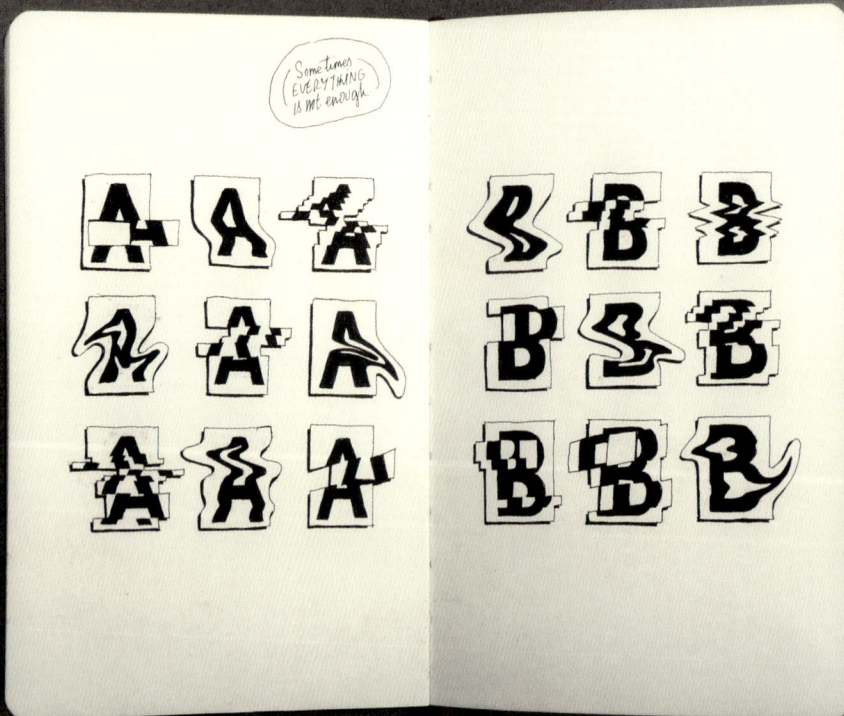

54

Easier said than Done!

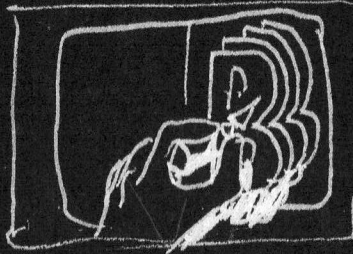

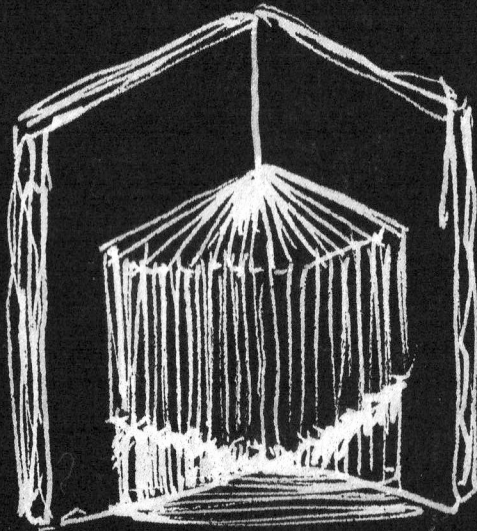

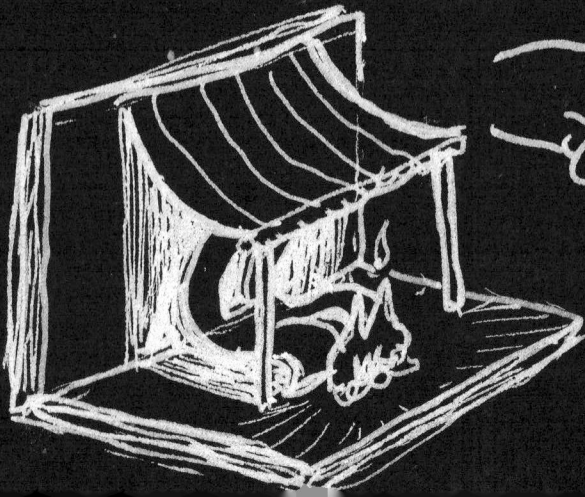

"Your eyes don't believe you."

SKETCHBOOK 2.0

"I start and finish with the sketchbook." Rylsee explains his creativity in terms of a terminally short attention span: "I think boredom is one of the keys of my creation. I get bored really easily, and this is why I always have my sketchbook to hand."

It is in the sketchbooks that Rylsee defined one of his signature styles. Continuing his exploration of analogue glitch and optical illusion, the designs are meant to scramble your eyes' relation to your brain. "These are some of my most visually disturbing works. Even though I created it myself, sometimes when I look at them, my eyes can't register if they are real or computer-generated."

And these illustrations break the fourth wall in more ways than one, by expanding out from the normally static dimensions of the notebook – some look like they come to-wards you, while others literally break away from the page.

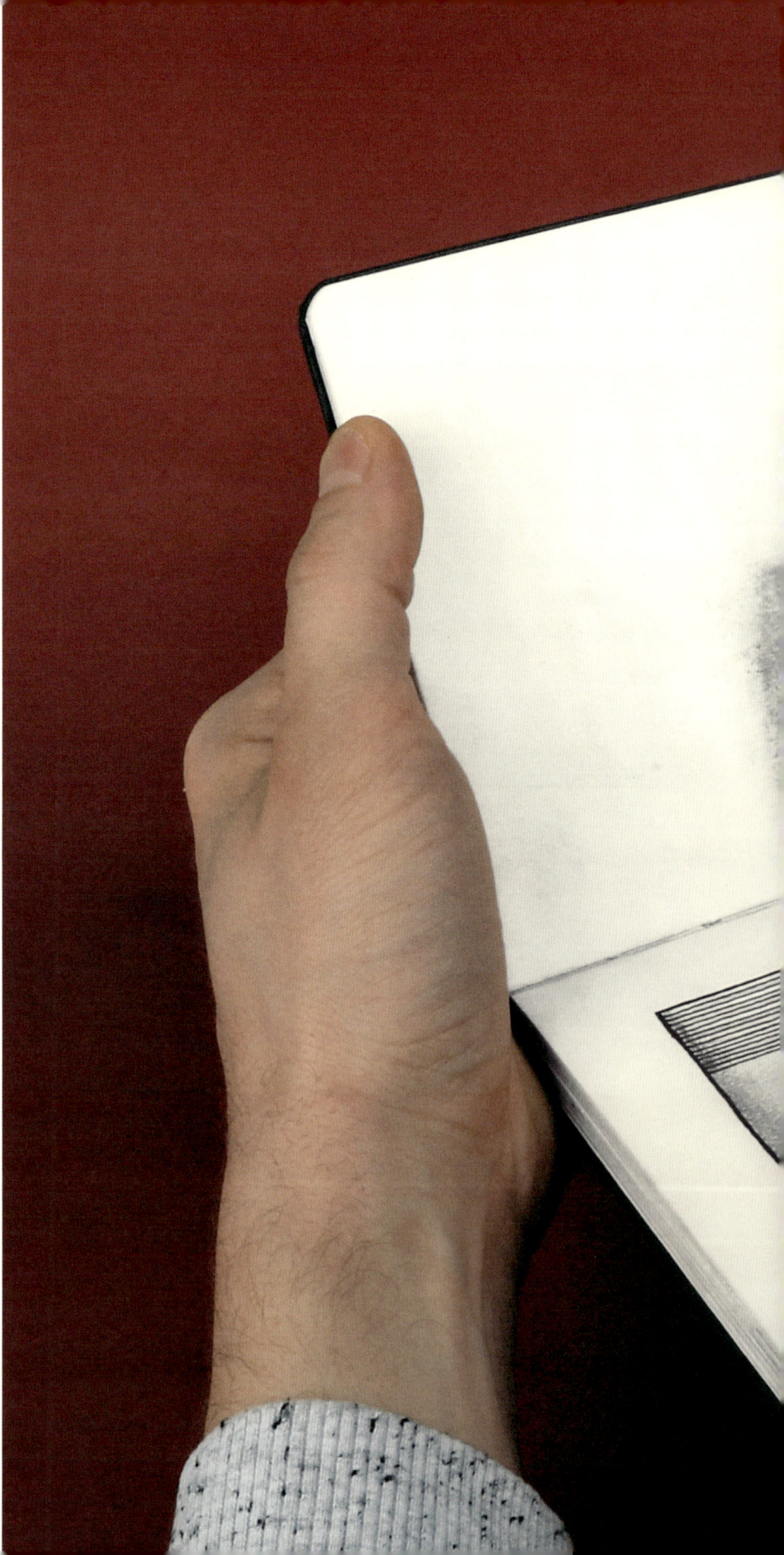

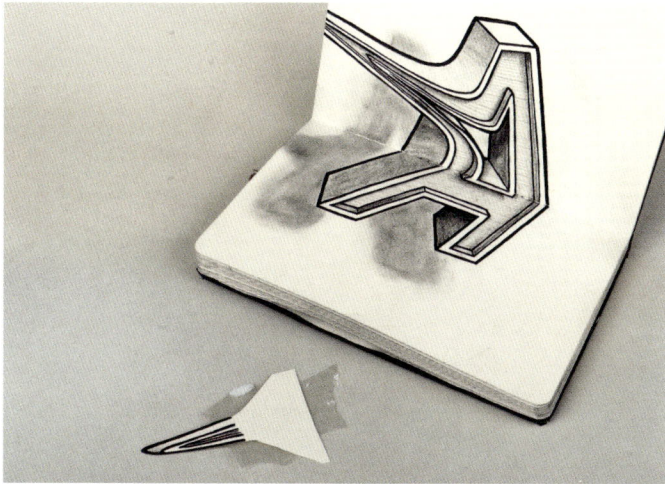

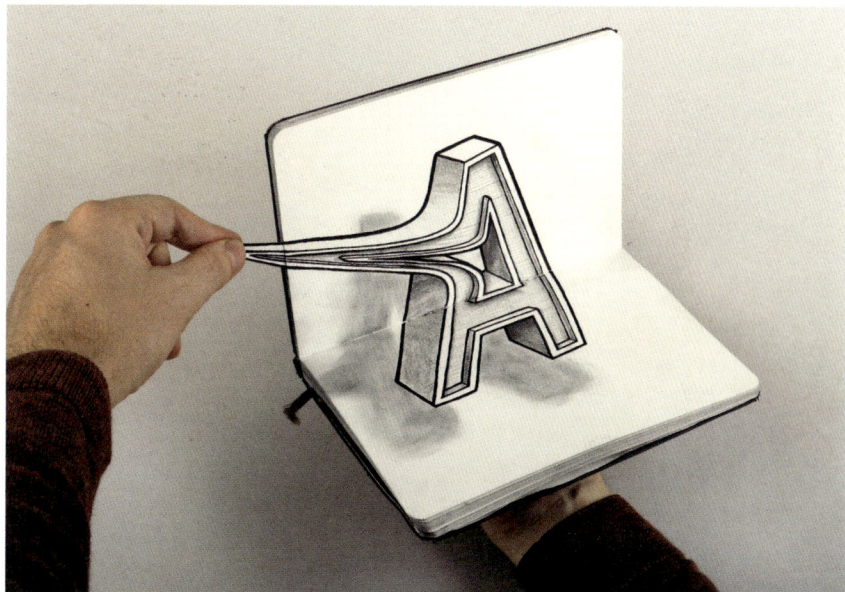

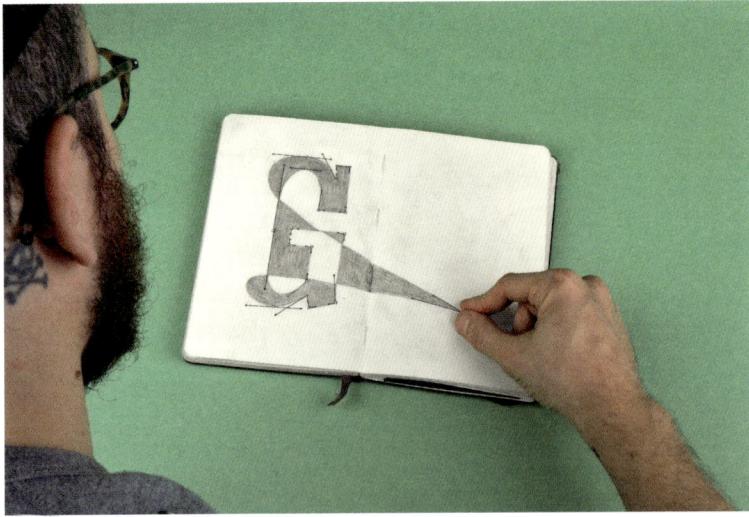

LOWERCASE MYSTERY (opposite): This illustration is a reference to the origin of the terms 'upper case' and 'lower case'. Simply, in the days when printing involved actual letters cast in iron, the capital letters were stored in the upper of two cases, and the smaller letters in the lower.

We live in a generation where deleting the history is more important than creating history

It's not until a mosquito lands on your testicles that you realize violence isn't the only answer.

WE LIVE IN A GENERAT

Peel it like a sticker

Year: 2014
Location: Berlin
Materials: Paper, Ink, Stop-motion

Sticker A is one of the first illustrations in the Sketchbook 2.0 project, which went viral in 2013 and has been immensely popular ever since. It arose from the idea of physical interaction with a drawing. It utilizes simple rules of perspective and shading. It also deploys the technique of anamorphosis, which works by creating an image that appears 3D, but only when seen from a certain vantage point (Holbein's painting The Ambassadors is the most famous use of this effect). The aim of this ongoing Sticker A project is to "play with the letter", to explore the technical and figurative properties of letters, as well as, in the words of the artist himself, "to push me to push the limits of my own mind." The 'A' is a favourite letter of Rylsee, who takes it as symbolic of beginnings.

68

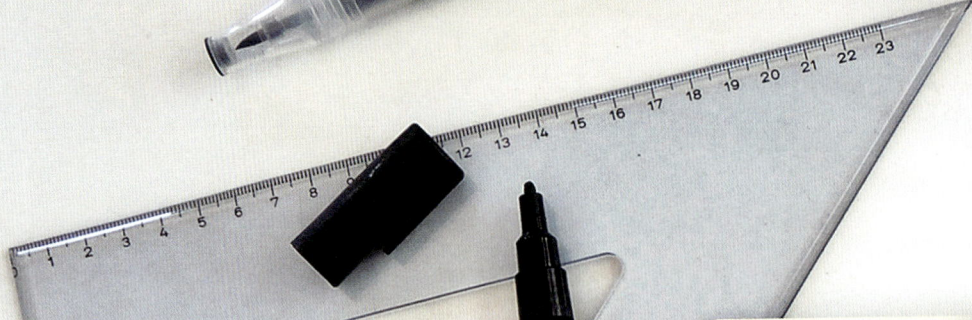

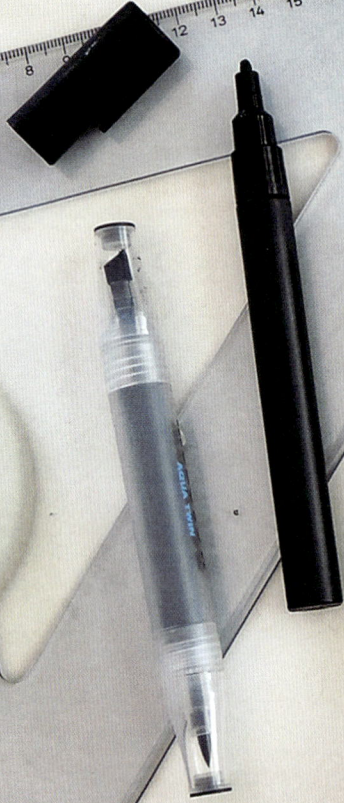

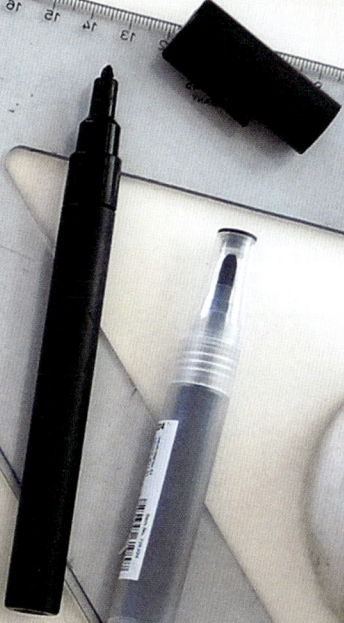

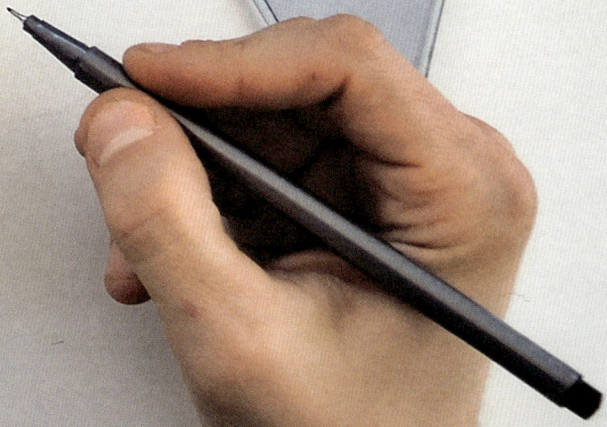

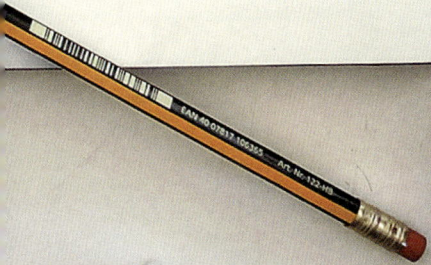

"The fake symmetry project was born after I began to see images appearing on Instagram that used what I supposed was a new app for creating mirrored images. People were using it with architecture to create trippy geometrical compositions. I'm always riffing on the idea of tricking people's eyes," Rylsee says, "and I decided that I would hand-make images like these ones, with the exception that my analogue images would contain mistakes or imperfections. Based on a central symmetrical axis, at first glance my images may just look like one of these Insta mirror effects, but when you take a closer look you can spot certain flaws. At this point, the image acquires a totally different dimension and the game is on!"

15. fev. 2014   Central bus station Tel-Aviv

16:21

I LOVE TEL-AVIV

16:26
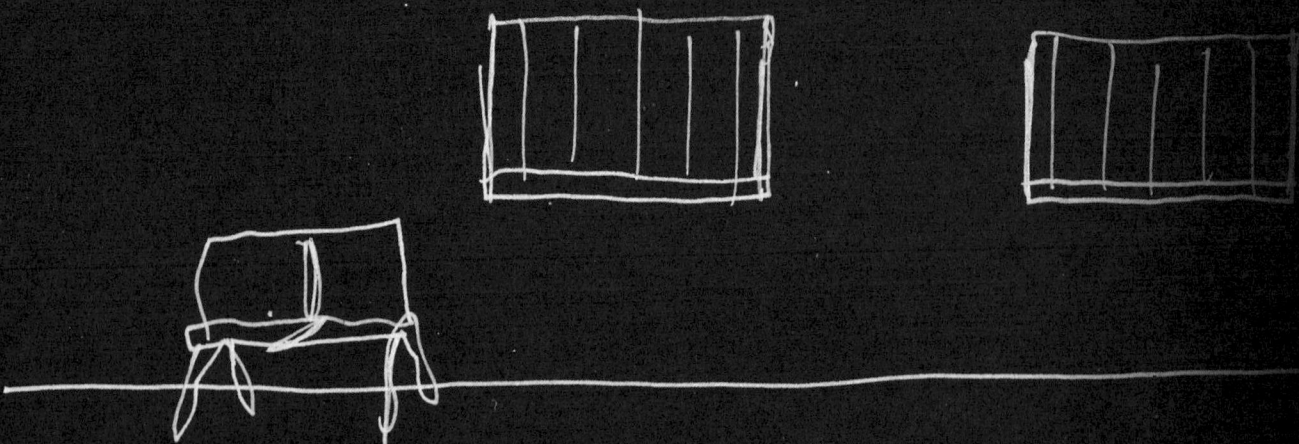

Clash   TAMAR

"Graffiti is choreography."

WALLS INSIDE AND OUT

Rylsee's work flourishes both in the gallery and outside in the wild. His street art pieces are known throughout the scene, and he has installed his artwork in cultural spaces from Chile to Tel Aviv. He brings a street-art-inspired wit to his installations, and intelligence and formal experimentation to his street pieces. While the style and approach may vary, an 'indoors' Rylsee piece is as recognizable as an 'outdoors' Rylsee piece. The common element, of course, is the wall.

"Graffiti is choreography. You have to learn it by hand, in order to do it fast, with style." Rooftops, ruined warehouses, storm drains or suburban walls – anywhere can become a canvas for Rylsee's typographical explorations. "Graffiti reflects the primal instinct of the male to mark territory. But I always saw an aesthetic in it."

What unifies all of Rylsee's big installations and interventions is the way they respond to architecture. Outdoors, he integrates architectonic elements into the composition of the piece, while indoors he always reacts to the space as fully as possible. With drawing, Rylsee says, there are only two elements: pen and paper. With a wall, however, the elements proliferate, taking in questions of space, location, time, and so on.

SAME AS IT NEVER WAS: Rylsee painted this mural in 2015, during the Springtime Delights Festival in La Rochelle, France. He had to draw on his years of experience as a graffiti writer. One challenge was logistical: the scaffolding they delivered him was only half the height of the wall, a problem he overcame with a skilful use of extensions and rollers. Another was compositional: the windows. "When you paint on a wall of uneven depth, you have to keep on stepping back from it to make sure the lines cross at the right spot. This is why I spent my weekend going up and down this half-scaffolding to make sure my font composition was looking right from across the street."

80

NEVER ENDING PLAYGROUND: This installation was for an exhibition in Geneva called RIDE THE WALL, a celebration of the intersection of street culture and skate culture. Alongside Rylsee, the exhibition featured big names like L'Atlas, Brokovich, Zest, not to mention three pieces by none other than Jean Michael Basquiat. Rylsee's installation is intended to be read as a narrative: "On the left, there's a curb with anti-skate on it, making the practice of the discipline impossible. The mirror reflecting the curb shows an imaginary continuity of the skate spot that is now dead. The signs on the wall indicate the change of mood. In the corner, I built a mountain with a cemetery at the bottom of it. Each tomb represents a skate spot in the city that has been killed with anti-skates. The last part of the installation features a skate deck cut into pixelated edges and connected to a TV screen and computer game. This represents the only option left to the youth once cities put these anti-skates everywhere."

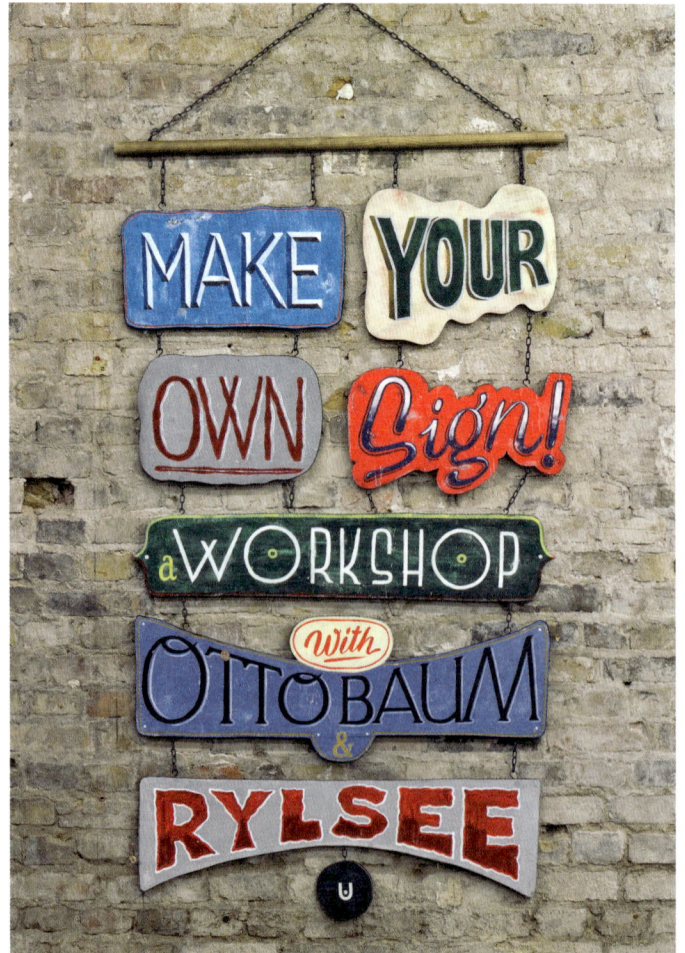

MYOS WORKSHOPS: In the words of Jim, Rylsee's friend from the Redgate project in Vancouver, "knowledge is one of the only things in life that you can share without dividing." This idea has resonated with Rylsee for a long time, and was in 2013 what sparked his setting up the MYOS (Make Your Own Sign) workshop series with friend Otto Baum. Otto and Rylsee are the perfect team, with Rylsee handling questions of composition and contemporary lettering, while Otto deals with the more traditional brush-lettering approach. "It's a positive circle," Rylsee says. "I teach other people, but it also helps me rethink my own working process. Sometimes when you do something for so long, you don't really think about how you do it anymore. But when I had to teach my techniques to people, I had to unpack my entire process in order to teach it properly. I realised that sharing my secret tricks makes me happy."

DISORGANIZED MESS: This piece was painted in the central bus station in Tel Aviv in 2014, in a building that was supposed to become the main shopping mall of the city. For some unknown reason, however, at some point construction just stopped, and today more than half the floors are unfinished and empty. Oddly, the bus station is at the top of the building, and here Rylsee spent an afternoon painting, alone but for a few odd figures drifting like zombies through the deserted mall.

AAAAAA: 'A' is for Annecy, a small city in France, and for the Art by Friends project, where Rylsee painted the AAAAAA wall during an art residency. This was in 2014, when he was "dissecting" letters a lot. The dissected 'A' is an illustration of the principle that you shouldn't judge a book by its cover: it is meant to represent a person's hidden depths, which only become visible when the person opens up.

INGLEWOOD: L'hamburger local opened in 2011 by two brothers, childhood friends of Rylsee, Inglewood is one of Switzerland's most renowned burger spots. He created the restaurant's entire visual identity, from the logo to the menus, the staff uniforms and the mural on the wall.

This piece was painted in summer 2015, as part of a group exhibition at Berlin's renowned Neurotitan gallery. The gallery is near Anne Frank's house, and there are often many tourists passing by. Rylsee describes how he was surprised to see how many people were taking selfies in front of the murals outside the gallery, rather than photos of the murals themselves. "This is when I remembered that I had the perfect sentence written in one of my sketchbooks: I WISH YOU COULD BE AS CUTE AS YOUR PROFILE PICTURE. This seemed like a pretty good spot for this slogan of mine."

Since then, this piece has become Rylsee's most tagged photo on Instagram, and the slogan is still there, despite being on one of Berlin's most coveted walls. People just love taking selfies with it, it seems. Ironic?

BATHROOM POETRY: 2013 saw Rylsee's
first solo show at the Square gallery
on his home turf of Geneva. The title
comes from the fact that many of the
artworks were inspired by graffiti
written in public bathrooms. The show
featured a range of slogans painted
on different materials, including wood
panels, paper and rusty metal.

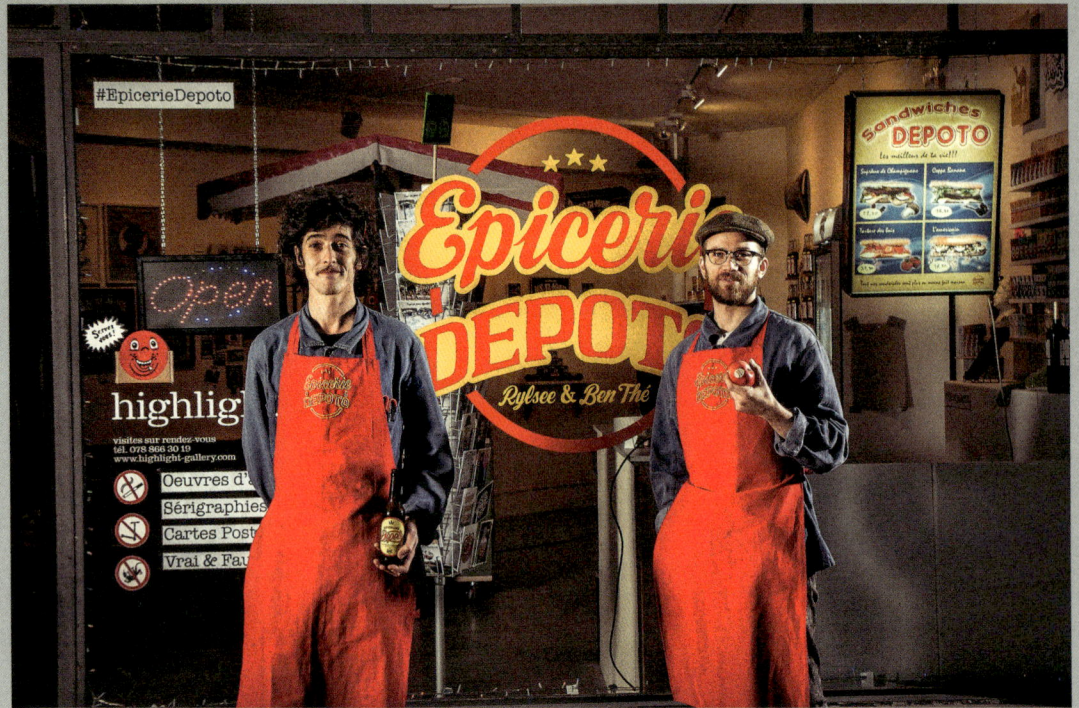

Épicerie Depoto

Year: November 2015 – February 2016
Location: Highligh Gallery, Geneva
Materials: Various

The Epicerie Depoto is the biggest piece Rylsee has made to date. A collaboration with Ben Thé, it involved the creation of a fake 'epicerie' or corner store in Geneva. The concept came to them when the gallery owner suggested they produce 'cheaper' pieces. The idea was to create, not just fake visuals, but a whole fake world for the store. Thus they made products, as well as labels, advertisements, packaging and even in-store displays, curating a whole boutique. They even filmed a fake TV commercial for their own brand of cigarettes. And, when they opened, the two artists put on a performance in which they acted the roles of corner store clerks. Rylsee gleefully describes how some people mistook the show for a real shop, while others came looking for the show, but assumed that the Epicerie Depoto was just another store.

HAIR DRYER A: This image is by far Rylsee's most popular to date, with over six thousand likes and countless comments. Instagram even included it in their annual book, and there is a lightbox of it at the Facebook/Instagram HQ in Dublin.

"This piece shows that when you do something honestly, without pretension and with love for what you do, at some point people will recognize your efforts," Ryslee says. "Internet magic," he adds, smiling.

The Vortex
Rylsee & Brokovich
Ride the Wall
2015

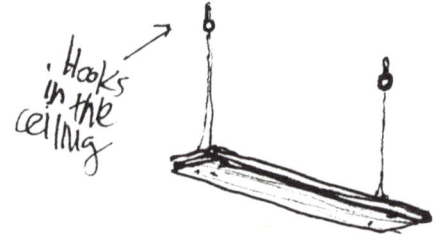

THE VORTEX: Rylsee was invited to be a guest artist at the 2015 edition of RIDE THE WALL. The organizers had invited him to collaborate with the artist Brokovich, a friend, on a mural. When he was exploring the space, however, Rylsee came across a pile of old wood on the roof, and inspiration struck. Despite the initial wariness of the organizers, this mindbending installation was a huge success.

I'VE NEVER RODE A BIKE

FASTER

VODIL 4OZ

STAY

E

Beginner's Luck

FLAT TIRE

A BAD MOMENT

SPEED

S

A Speed

Mister OZ

Biker Poser

Wheels

Devils

"Look better."

FASHION, ETC.

Another thing that defines Rylsee is his restlessness. Constantly urged by an impulse of motion, he explores new ways to share his work with people and develop practices to take in new media and platforms. His collaboration with Nike on marketing materials is an example where Rylsee finds a way to have a wider audience exposed to his work together with the possibility of exploring the potential of a new medium. It can also be discerned in his recent opening of the clothing and accessory brand Sneeer. In retrospect, this step seems logical. For Rylsee the whole world is a canvas, and anything from billboards to crash helmets can be transformed into a vehicle for his idiosyncratic vision. One of the most exciting aspects of these newer projects is that they show how well that vision translates to less conventional formats, while retaining its essential nature.

Toujours
Difficile
Super
STINKY
Now or Never
BIENSÛR
HELLO
MY BACK is FUCKED
Once Again
ACTUALLY
DEMAIN
Tomorrow
REEFER Lover
GET
INSTAGRAM
NEVER ENDING
WINTER
WORD!
TOO FANCY
EXTRA
ALMOST
COFFEIN
TOO INTENSE
AMAZED
BORING
NON
SNOOZE
YOU LOSE
HIT
RUSH
REMEMBER
THIS WAY
MAIS MEC
FAST
FEELING
FAIR
.RYLSEE 2013
49/100

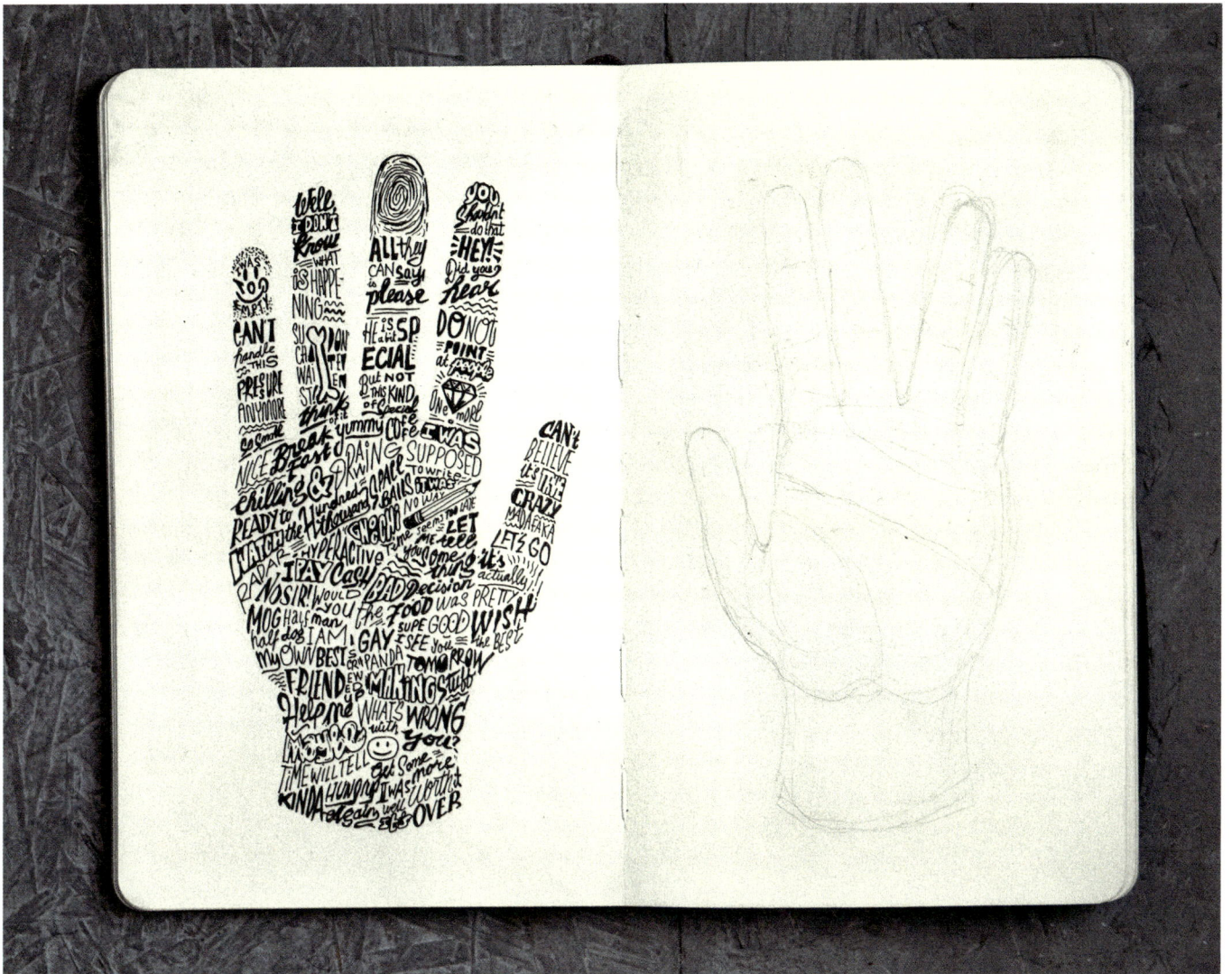

OPEN DIARY: According to Rylsee, "this artwork was on my studio table the whole time I was preparing for an exhibition." Each message was drawn using a freehand font. "It is a 'recording' of all the things that got my attention during the making of it, from thoughts, to music lyrics, jokes and onomatopoeias. I wrote down everything as it came."

This print was conceived for the exhibition Bathroom Poetry at The Square, Geneva. The Original artwork was drawn with Ink on paper (100x70cm). The print was an A1 offset print, in a limited edition of 100, signed and numbered.

FASHION, ETC.

WHERE THE WIND BLOWS: Handpainted Biltwell helmet for the group exhibition / art auction DC Brain Cover.

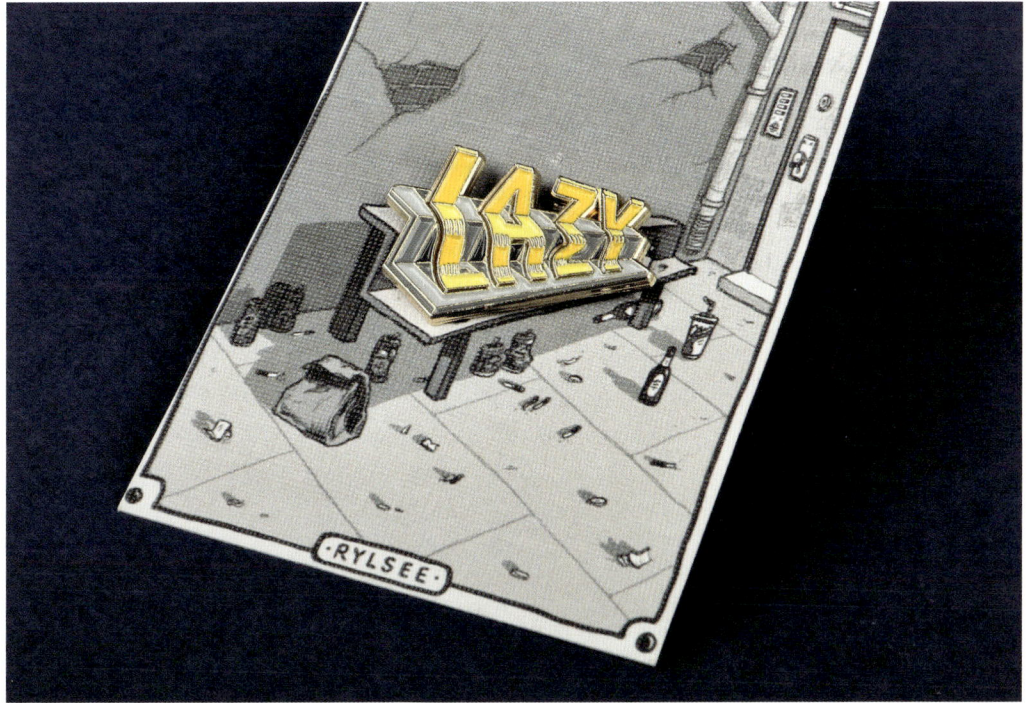

LAZY PIN: Limited edition pin based on
one of Rylsee's paintings. Manufactured
by StupidKrap for the exhibition Pinzil-
la in Melbourne and L.A.

Sneeer clothing

Year: 3015 - ongoing
Location: Berlin
Materials: Clothing and apparel

The clothing label Sneeer is a very recent project that Rylsee set up with his brother Yann at the end of 2015. The range manages to combine frontline street style with an unmistakably Rylsee aesthetic, translating some of his most well known riffs to caps and t-shirts. It is also a chance for Rylsee to collaborate with musicians, creating collectible band t-shirts based on their lyrics and visual universe.

NIKE - JUST DID IT: For Rylsee, col-laborating with Nike on three illus-tration series in 2014, was a dream come true: "After reading an email from the senior art director of Nike world, telling me that his team has been following my work for a while, I nearly fainted."

URBAN SPREE T-SHIRTS: The first design (following spread, left) was inspired by Rylsee's stay in "sleepless" Sao Paulo, specifically by Pixação, a graffiti style native to the city. "If I had to explain it in two words I would say that it is somewhere between tagging and parkour," Rylsee explains. "Pixação pushes the limits of graffiti. Every crew develops its own alphabet. Most of them have spikey shapes which give Pixação this unique aesthetic. The impressive thing is that the competition between crews is not only based on how much they

tag, but on how high up they do it: you can see whole buildings covered from top to bottom in these enigmatic symbols." In Berlin the Berlin Kidz/ ÜF crew have developed a style that is influenced by Pixação.

The second design (following spread, right) shows the main logo of Urban Spree. It went from a design for a sticker to adorning the entrance to Urban Spree and the signature t-shirt of the cultural centre. Designed by Rylsee and printed at the legendary Mother Drucker screen print studio, both t-shirts are 100% Urban Spree.

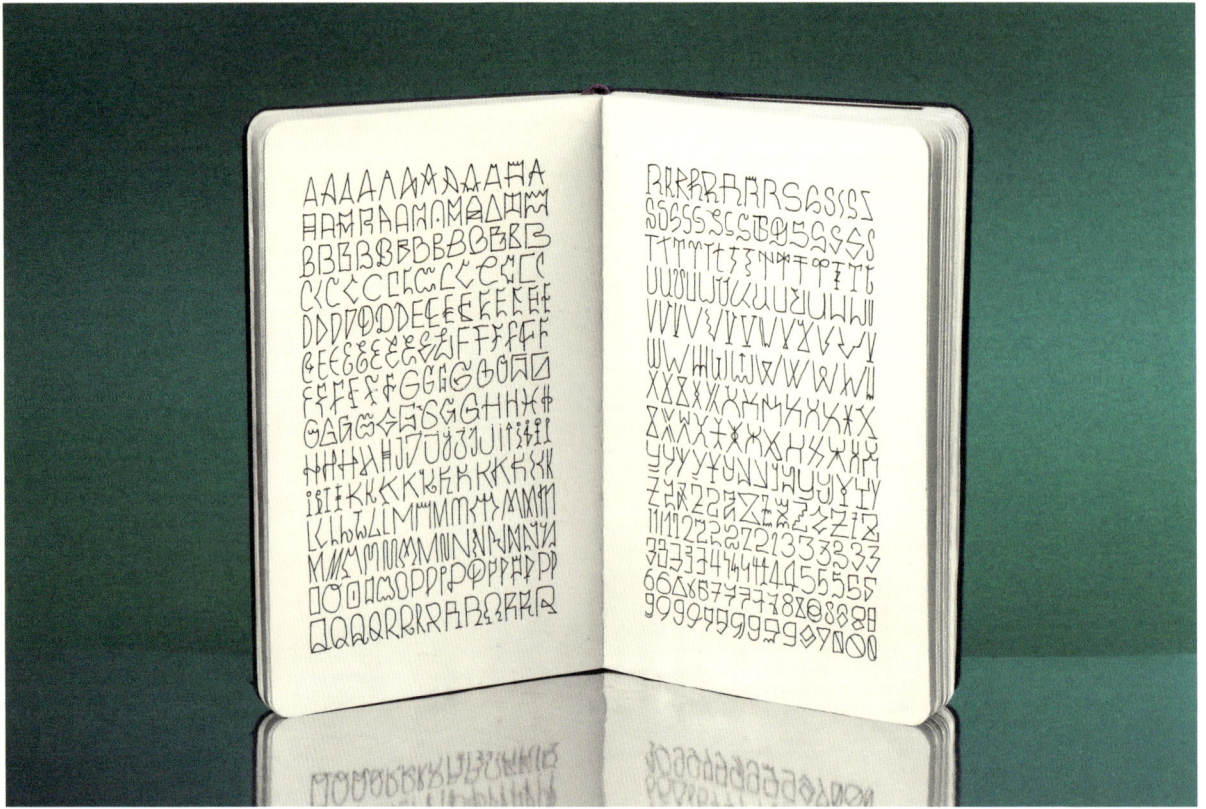

Photo credits

PP. 9, 74
Andrea Wan

PP. 10-11
Laurent Xavier Moulin

P. 13
Zosen

PP. 80-81 (unknown)

P. 83
Secret of happiness by
Nicolas Schopfer

P. 84 (bottom right)
Otto Baum

P. 85
Pascal Gautherot

PP. 86, 90, 93 (bottom right)
Gabriel Balagué

P. 88
Nicolas Schopfer
(Frames and Gallery view)

P. 105 (bottom right)
Art direction: Rommy González
Photo: Maansi Jain

PP. 12, 21, 32, 33, 40, 41, 46, 47, 48,
49, 53, 55, 56, 57, 68 (bottom), 71,
72-73, 75, 76, 77, 81, 82, 83 (right),
86, 87, 88 (bottom left), 91, 92, 94,
95, 96, 97, 102, 103 (bottom), 104,
105 (top)
Cyril Vouilloz aka Rylsee

PP. 16, 17, 18-19, 20, 24, 25, 30, 31,
38, 39, 42, 43, 50-51, 54, 60-61, 62,
63, 64, 65, 68 (top), 69, 70, 92 (bottom), 95 (bottom), 100, 101, 103 (top),
107, 108, 109, 111
Luca Bogoni

Thanks! Ü

Dedicated to my daughter Alma

Spécial Thanks to:
Urban spree family, Luca Bogoni, Memo Vithana,
Rommy González, Roberto Di Puma, John Z. komurki,
My mom & Gilda, Yann Vouilloz, Andrea Wan, Ben Thé, Gabee,
Otto baum, Addison Karl, Low bros, Hiroyatzu Tsuri (Twoone),
Johannes Mundinger, David Walker, Klone, Pascal & Vero
Feucher, Nico Defawe, Frédéric Wickström, Josh Murphy,
Dolly Demoratti, Justine Bonie, Elisabetta Pajer, Zero cents,
Eli Robat, Editude Pictures (Andy & Fredi), Onio, Alex Canana,
Mathieu Jacquesson, Benoit B Barraud, Amparo Catnapp,
Manon & Nathan Vouilloz, Art by friends (Camille Renaudin),
Thomas Brokovich, Affenfaust Gallery Hamburg, Springtime
Delights Festival (Antoine Robert), Ride the wall (Anouck,
Lena, Claudine), Erica Vicente, Delio Waled Fiores, The square
Geneva, Inglewood (Maïko, Bastien, Maurice, Loris),
The workshop (Raph & Alex), Estelle Spirig, Christian Krueger,
Pascal Gautherot, Neurotitan Gallery Berlin (Anika),
Nicolas Schopfer, Maansi Jain, Zosen, Red Gate (Vancouver),
The Art Union (Diana, Boogie, Philipp), Laurent Xavier moulin,
Mathgoth Gallery Paris (Mathilde & Gautier), La Vallée Brussels
(Pierre Pevée), Hell'o collective, Jim Zbinden (Pulp 68),
Chris Digs (NIKE), Aaron (Stupid Krap), Épicerie Depoto,
Highlight Gallery Geneva, Roland Gueissaz,
Yann Schmidthalter, Xavier Ripolles, Gabriel Bonnefoy,
Fabio Poujouly, Nicolas Haenni, Xav DAB2, Loïc Benoit,
Thomas & Manu Müller, Go Out Mag (Mina & Mabrouk),
Instagrafite (Marcelo & Marina), Capsule Gallery
(Carole Rigaut), Bar du nord, Couleur 3

...all my G's around the globe!

...And all the people who have been supporting me all these
years, you know who you are! <3